Jesse Jackson

JESSE JACKSON

ANNA KOSOF

FRANKLIN WATTS
NEW YORK/LONDON/TORONTO/SYDNEY/1987

Frontis photograph courtesy of
AP/Wide World Photos.

Photographs courtesy of: Copyrighted,
Chicago Today, All rights reserved, used
with permission: pp. 18 (top), 20 (top);
Barbara A. Reynolds & JFJ Associates,
Washington, D.C.: pp. 18 (bottom left and right),
20 (bottom), 23 (top, bottom left and center);
Sterling High School Yearbook, 1959: p. 23
(bottom right); AP/Wide World Photos: pp. 32,
36, 43, 45, 101; Sygma: pp. 51 (Ira Wyman),
60 (Owen Franklin); UPI/Bettmann Newsphotos:
pp. 65, 72, 81, 82 (Reuters), 95.

Library of Congress Cataloging-in-Publication Data

Kosof, Anna.

Jesse Jackson

Bibliography: p.
Includes index.
Summary: A biography of the black Presidential
candidate in 1984 who is a major leader of Afro-
Americans today.
1. Jackson, Jesse, 1941-   —Juvenile literature.
2. Afro-American—Biography—Juvenile litereraure.
3. Civil rights workers—United States—Biography—
Juvenile literature. 4. Presidential candidates—
United States—Biography—Juvenile literature.
5. Afro-Americans—Civil rights—Juvenile literature.
[1. Jackson, Jesse, 1941-   . 2. Afro-Americans—
Biography] I. Title.
E185.97.J25K67 1987 973.92′092′ 4 [B] [92] 87-10500
ISBN 0-531-10413-3

I would like to thank the
Reverend Jesse L. Jackson for
his time and his cooperation.
I would also like to express
my thanks to Jack O'Dell and
Barbara Reynolds, whose help
has been invaluable.

Contents

Introduction
11

Chapter One
Growing Up Black
17

Chapter Two
Emergence of a Leader
27

Chapter Three
PUSH
41

Chapter Four
Chicago Years
53

Chapter Five
Run, Jesse, Run
63

Chapter Six
Jackson's Foreign
Affairs Policies
75

Chapter Seven
Jesse L. Jackson,
the Man
87

Chapter Eight
Jackson's Impact
on American Life
97

Sources
103

Index
109

Jesse Jackson

Introduction

Jesse Jackson's story is, in many ways, the story of one of the most important eras of the civil rights movement. To examine the complexity and evolution of Jesse Jackson is to look closely at the progression and changes in the movement in the 1960s, 1970s, and 1980s.

This man, who coined the phrase "I am somebody," has passionately demonstrated he is just that— a somebody, a force to be reckoned with. He has repeatedly said, "I want to be respected and heard . . . the issues I raise and the constituency I represent won't go away."

The political beginnings of Jesse Jackson are hard to pinpoint, but one thing is certain. History was dramatically changed when Dr. Martin Luther King, Jr., was assassinated on April 4, 1968, and Jackson moved to the forefront of the black fight for equality.

It was an anxious time. Since 1965 the civil rights movement had gained momentum in the South. Marches and confrontations with the police were telecast to the nation on the nightly news. Civil rights workers were being beaten and tear-gassed by the police, and arrested or jailed for attempting to integrate restaurants, rest rooms, schools, and buses. On March 28, 1968, Dr. King, head of the Southern Christian Leadership Conference (SCLC), arrived in Memphis to lead a march through the downtown section in support of striking sanitation workers.

April 3, 1968, was a strangely prophetic day. To a cheering crowd at the local Baptist church, Dr. King delivered what some people believe to be one of the finest speeches ever made. He spoke eloquently, with repeated references to his own premature death—he "had been to the mountain top." What the audience heard in his message was that he was prepared to die. It was as if he foresaw the tragedy that would take place the next day.

Jesse Jackson, the twenty-six-year-old civil rights worker, was also in Memphis, to assist Dr. King, his mentor and teacher. Jackson was an ambitious organizer and one of the youngest associated with the legendary civil rights leader.

At 6:01 P.M. on April 4, 1968, Martin Luther King was shot on the balcony of the Lorraine Motel. His associates tried to telephone for an ambulance, but ironically the switchboard operator died of a heart attack at the same time the shot was fired that killed King.

Dr. King's death left the nation in shock and deep mourning. While most of the SCLC staff stayed in their motel rooms, stunned by the loss of their leader, Jesse Jackson spoke to the press. Jackson's action was bold. Only a junior member of the SCLC, he was not as close to King as Dr. Ralph Abernathy, King's right-hand man, or Andrew Young, who went on to become ambassador to the United Nations and then mayor of Atlanta. Jackson's actions that evening have been condemned by people both inside and outside the civil rights movement. Some have called him "an opportunist of the most cynical kind." That night he demonstrated his unerring ability to get the media's attention. While his colleagues were in mourning, he seized the leadership of the civil rights movement, knowing that it desperately needed a spokesperson.

On the night that King died, many large cities erupted in violence. Fires raged in the ghettos. As the funeral arrangements were being made for Dr. King in Memphis, Jackson left for Chicago. Dr. Abernathy had given Jackson permission to leave, assuming that he was going to Chicago to organize people to fly to Memphis for the funeral.

By the time Jackson landed in Chicago, riots had broken out, and black youths were looting and smashing windows. Fires eventually destroyed more than a million dollars' worth of property and left over a thousand people homeless. Allegedly breaking an agreement with King's people not to talk to the press, less than twelve hours after King's death, Jackson appeared on *The Today Show*. In Memphis, according to some who stayed with King's body, they watched helplessly as this young newcomer to King's SCLC spoke for the organization. Some felt that he had "not paid his dues," had not shared the years in jail by King's side, as Ralph Abernathy had. Earlier, King himself had designated Abernathy as his successor in the event of his death.

Jesse Jackson sat in the NBC studios wearing the same sweater and slacks he had worn the evening before. But now the sweater was soaked with blood—that of Dr. King. How the blood got onto his sweater is still in dispute. Some people called it a media stunt, some would not comment. But one thing was indisputable—while King's men were distraught, silent, and numbed, Jesse Jackson appeared on national television and spoke to the American people about the tragedy.

Addressing the city council of Chicago later that day, still wearing the blood-smeared sweater, he declared, "I am calling for nonviolence . . . in the homes, on the streets, in the classrooms and in our relationships with one another. I'm challenging the youth of today to be nonviolent as the greatest expression of faith they can make to Dr. King—to put your rocks down, put your bottles down." It was a message America needed and wanted to hear.

At that time the Black Panthers, the Student Nonviolent Coordinating Committee (SNCC), and other radical groups were feared and distrusted. In contrast, Jackson was charismatic. His voice fluctuated like that of Dr. King's; his words were conciliatory. In a time of such confusion and turmoil, a voice that could bring people together and offer an alternative to violence was one that attracted the media.

Jackson looked fierce, but his message was one of nonviolence. He was articulate, spoke eloquently, and possessed the physical appearance with which black America could identify. His message was acceptable to most people. He was a person with whom they could talk.

The Black Panthers were calling for race riots and more radical solutions to discrimination. But some felt that if this person who advocated nonviolence and peace was killed, then what hope was there for the rest of black America? The old guard, represented by Ralph Abernathy from the SCLC, Roy Wilkins from the NAACP (the National Association for the Advancement of Colored People), and Whitney Young from the National Urban League, advocated nonviolence. But to those living in the terrible conditions of the ghettos, this approach seemed out of step with reality. It represented an older generation of leaders they could no longer follow.

In this sense, King's death seemed the last straw, and it was in such an atmosphere that Jesse Jackson emerged as a leader. He seemed to offer an alternative compromise between those considered to be out of touch with black America and those who advocated violence and destruction to end racial discrimination.

The media were drawn to Jackson. He looked militant, yet he spoke in measured tones. He photographed well, as he talked about the pride of black America.

Had history taken a different turn, Jesse Jackson might not have had the opportunity to assume leadership. If one of the more senior staff members of the SCLC had stepped into that role with the same charisma and style, Jackson might not have emerged as a major spokesperson. But at a very young age, still in his late twenties, he became a leader.

Today, the Reverend Jesse Jackson is considered this nation's best-known black American. Some people regard him as the most powerful black person in the world. He has appeared on the covers of *Time* and *Newsweek*. He has appeared on more television programs than any other black in America, except for entertainers. He is the only black American ever to wage a "serious" campaign for the presidency of the United States of America.

A statesman without portfolio, he has been welcomed by Pope John Paul II, the Archbishop of Canterbury, Palestine Liberation Organization leader Yasser Arafat, Cuban leader Fidel Castro, and by dozens of heads of state in Africa and the Western world.

In 1969, he was proclaimed by *Playboy* magazine "King's heir apparent." In 1984, he received over three and a half million votes for president without one television ad.

Yet, he is a complicated person, loved by many but disliked by others.

Who is this man who has captured America's imagination, who, according to Gallup polls, is held in high esteem, surpassed only by the Pope and President Ronald Reagan?

Who is Jesse Jackson?

1
Growing Up Black

"Today, when you hear him say, 'I am somebody,' to motivate others, you wouldn't believe how long he was saying that to himself," Mrs. Xanthene Norris, Jackson's high school French teacher, recalled.

On October 8, 1941, a seven-pound, four-ounce baby boy was brought into this world by a midwife. She remembers the event vividly. "It seemed that the child was in a hurry to get there. By the time the doctor arrived, I had just wrapped him in a blanket and laid him in bed with his mother."

Jesse Louis Burns was born in Greenville, South Carolina, to a teenager, Helen Burns. His father, Noah Robinson, a married man with three children, lived next door. Robinson never married Jesse's mother.

Naming this child was a serious event. "Jesse" came from Noah Robinson's father, the Reverend Jesse Robinson, who, along with his twin brother, Jacob, was a Baptist minister. The two preachers were first-generation descendants of Cherokee Indians. Reverend Jesse Robinson's wife was a slave, whose father was an Irish plantation owner and the sheriff of Greenville County about 1850. "With all that Irish

This house in Greenville, South Carolina, was the birthplace of Jesse Jackson on October 8, 1941.

Jesse at age two months (above), and (right) two and a half years

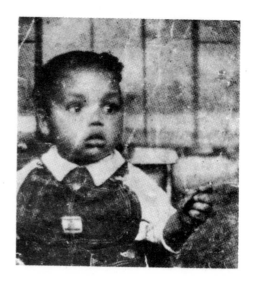

blood running through his veins, no wonder Jesse is hot-tempered and always on a war path," his father has said. Mr. Robinson, a handsome, no-nonsense man, fully acknowledged responsibility for his son. He was known to brag, "Yup, that's my boy and he's the spitting image of me."

It is not certain when Jesse became fully aware of the circumstances of his birth. According to Noah, Jesse's half-brother and ten months his junior, he discovered that Jesse was his brother when one day someone whispered in his ear, "See that kid over there with the curly hair? Well, he's your brother." At first, Noah did not believe the "vicious lie," but his father never denied the rumor. Noah, Jr., grew up next door to Jesse Jackson, but not until high school did they attend the same school.

When Jesse was two years old, his mother married Charles Henry Jackson, who legally adopted Jesse. His stepfather, Charles Jackson, recalled, "I never told him I was not his father, because I didn't want him to grow up thinking he was different." However, apparently Jesse was deeply affected by his circumstances and was hurt by not having his real father at home. Watching the family next door, seeing his stepbrother Noah play with his father, made him feel rejected and left out.

GROWING UP BLACK

From all indications, Jesse was a very sensitive and aggressive child. As a childhood friend recalled, "One thing that I remember about Jesse was his inquisitiveness. He always used to ask why. He questioned the rules at a time when everybody else had accepted them because they had always been that way."

At a very early age, he had become aware of things around him that many children would not

Left: Noah Ryan Robinson,
Jesse's *half-brother*, and, right,
Noah Louis Robinson, Jesse's father.
Below: Helen and Charles Jackson,
Jesse's mother and stepfather

notice. "All the little homes we used to live in," he recalled, "were owned by an old man named Mr. Hellum, who used to come around on Saturday afternoons in his little old truck to collect the rent. He was white, and he'd come around with his little book and those that didn't have the rent money would be running and hiding in the bushes and acting like they weren't home and he'd be chasing them to collect the rent. They were filled with fear and I always resented that."

Greenville, where Jackson grew up, was a segregated Southern town until the early 1960s. Jesse grew up knowing that he was expected to be subservient and inferior to whites. As a boy, the Colored or Whites Only signs were a constant, hurtful reminder that the two races were kept separate. He once recalled, "We would say we didn't want to eat because we weren't hungry, or we didn't want to drink water because we weren't thirsty or we didn't want to go to the movie theater because we didn't want to see the picture. Actually we were lying because we were afraid."

Jesse's grandmother, his mother's mother, was a significant member of the family. "Aunt Tibby," as she was affectionately called, couldn't read or write, but she had a profound impact on Jesse's life. It was she who instilled in him the belief that he was somebody.

"For God's sake, Jesse, promise me you'll be somebody. Ain't no such word as *cain't*. *Cain't* got drowned in the soda bottle. Don't let the Joneses get you down. Nothing is impossible for those who have the Lord. Come hell or high water, if you got the guts, boy, ain't nothing or nobody can turn you around," she used to say.

Those words struck a note in Jesse's mind. The same philosophy was later echoed in the message he preached to the youth of America.

From the age of six, he always had some kind of job. The family was not poor, but work was important in the Southern ethic and seriously promoted in the Jackson family. The saying "An idle mind is the devil's workshop" was a hard-and-fast rule. His first job was with his grandmother's friend, Mr. Summers. He helped to pick up lumber slabs, saw them into firewood, and then deliver them in the neighborhood. He was the first black child to sell concessions at Greenville's Whites Only football stadium. At ten, he was shining shoes at his stepfather's shoe-shine parlor. He continued to work all through high school in all types of jobs, from caddying at the Greenville Country Club, to collecting tickets at the Liberty Theatre, to cleaning machinery at a bakery on the weekends.

THE DRIVE TO EXCEL

While the Jacksons were not poor, both Jesse and his other half-brother, born to his mother and stepfather, worked at odd jobs, supplementing the family's income. His stepfather was a post office worker and his mother a beautician.

Traditional values like hard work and striving for excellence were instilled in him at home, at school and at church. His teachers remember him as "always being number one in everything." They called him a "fierce competitor, a charmer with an uncanny drive to prove himself." Today, the same qualities stand out.

When he was only nine, he was elected to the National Sunday School Convention in Charlotte, his first public-speaking engagement.

In high school Jackson ran for whatever school office was open. In the ninth grade he was elected president of his class and president of the honor society. Xanthene Norris, his French teacher, noted, "He

Above: *as a teenager growing up in Greenville,
Jesse lived in this house. Below (from left to right):
Jesse at age ten, fourteen, and seventeen*

was ambitious and excelled through hard work. Jesse was always the candidate." She added, "Jesse never complained, never made excuses for himself, never wallowed in self-pity."

Sports also had a major impact on his early development. Jackson was an excellent athlete. At Sterling High School, the coach considered him the best quarterback he had ever trained. His coach always emphasized the connection between physical excellence and intellectual pursuits. This same concept has governed Jackson's life, and whenever he speaks to young audiences, you can hear him say, "Big muscles alone won't get you there, you must also know how to read and write to make it in this society."

Early in life, he was confronted with blatant racism. Upon graduation from Sterling High School in Greenville in 1959, the star athlete was offered a contract to play baseball for the New York Giants. The American League's Chicago White Sox countered the bid and offered Jackson $6,000 to play for them instead. It seemed a great offer, but then Jackson discovered that a white ballplayer had received an offer of $90,000 from the same club! He refused to accept. It seemed like a slap in the face.

Instead of playing major-league ball, he accepted an athletic scholarship to the University of Illinois in Chicago. But this period in the North was discouraging. Northern racism seemed to surpass what he had known and seen in Greenville. He was shattered to learn that in the North he could not be quarterback, a position reserved for whites only. In 1963, uncomfortable with the division between black and white students on campus and generally unhappy at the University of Illinois, Jackson returned South to the black Agriculture and Technical College of North Carolina at Greensboro. There he became a star quarterback on the football team and won numerous honors. During this time he met Jacqueline Davis, a fellow student, and they married.

COMING INTO
THE MOVEMENT

Jackson arrived in Greensboro at the beginning of the historic sit-ins in the South. His timing could not have been better. As a leader on campus, with speaking ability, the star quarterback organized boycotts of segregated restaurants and theaters. He joined the Congress of Racial Equality (CORE), a major civil rights organization, and started organizing sit-ins in Greensboro. For ten months, Jackson organized and led demonstrations.

His efforts to desegregate Greensboro did not go unnoticed. In recognition of his accomplishments he was elected president of the newly created North Carolina Intercollegiate Council on Human Rights. By his senior year, he took a leadership position in CORE. He became the field director of Southeastern operations, a role that took him deeper into the civil rights struggle and indirectly led him to work with Dr. Martin Luther King, Jr.

Jesse's roommate at school recalled a strange event in Jesse's life. "One night, he woke up and said he had an odd dream. He said that he thought he had been called to preach. He was shaking. I never saw him look so serious before."

After obtaining a bachelor's degree in sociology, he accepted a Rockefeller grant to the Chicago Theological Seminary. During that time, Jackson was torn between the ministry and the protest movement. He considered going to Duke University's law school, but chose the ministry instead because, he said, he believed that the cloistered environment of the seminary would enable him to reflect and meditate away from turmoil. It didn't turn out that way. Chicago became his new home, and it was to have a major impact on the shape of his life for the next fifteen years.

The civil rights movement—the sit-ins, marches, and confrontations—interfered with the "peaceful reflection" in the seminary. Watching television in his dormitory, Jackson saw police use tear gas and whips on women and children. Outraged, he organized half the student body to make the drive to Selma, Alabama, where he had his first opportunity to meet his hero, Dr. King, and talk with him in person.

Andrew Young remembered Jackson as "merely a face in the crowd of thousands who poured into Selma in 1965 when King issued a call for foot soldiers.

"I remember getting a little annoyed," Young said, "because Jesse was giving orders from the steps of Brown Chapel and nobody knew who he was. All the other marchers came up getting in line, but Jesse, assuming a staff role, automatically started directing the marchers. I also remember him telling me what a great pamphlet I wrote, *The Bible and the Ballot*. I was really flattered. It sort of took the edge off."

Betty Washington, a reporter for the *Chicago Daily Defender*, was also at Selma. She recalled, "I thought it strange that he would make a speech, when he was not on the SCLC staff and had not been included in any of the strategy meetings. He just seemed to have come from nowhere. Like, who was he? But he spoke so well, I recorded his statement anyway. I had the feeling that one day he might be important."

It was Ralph Abernathy, who later became the president of the SCLC, who encouraged a reluctant King to hire the young man. Reverend Abernathy was impressed with the tremendous organizing talents that Jackson had exhibited very early on.

That's how Jesse Jackson, a young man still in graduate school, made his presence felt and found a place with Dr. King.

2
Emergence of a Leader

If the Civil War of the 1860s decided whether or not this country would tolerate slavery, the civil rights movement of the 1960s questioned whether a segregated and unequal society would go unchallenged. One of the chief catalysts behind that challenge was Dr. Martin Luther King, Jr.

With his nonviolent approach, Dr. King waged a battle for desegregation in the South during the early sixties. He pressed for integration in schools, restaurants, and housing, and equal access to public water fountains and rest rooms.

Dr. King was very effective in the South. He understood the Southern culture; he knew how to make the system respond to pressure. By the mid-sixties he was ready to take his movement to other areas, and it seemed important to address the problems of the Northern urban ghettos. In the North, with its densely populated pockets of poverty, segregation was enforced without the Colored Only or Whites Only signs. King was a stranger to these areas, but to Jackson, the Northern ghettos were becoming familiar territory. His earlier stay as a student in Chicago opened his eyes to a different way of life. The North could not be organized like the South. The people, the problems, and the issues were different from those in the South. Colored Only signs were absent. Theoretically, blacks could eat in restaurants or live wherever they pleased, but in reality, they were as segregated, in many ways, as blacks in the South. King knew he needed a national base of operation and he selected Chicago as the city to provide him that opportunity. He viewed Chicago as the capital of Northern segregation. The year was 1966 and the time had come to deal with the North. When King arrived in July, Jackson was there to meet him, already very much involved in the fight for black equality.

CHICAGO'S MIGHTY MAYOR

Chicago mayor Richard Daley was already a legend. Perhaps one of the most powerful mayors in the nation, he proudly declared that Chicago did not have any segregation. "We recognize every man, regardless of race, national origin and creed." With the mayor's denial that the ghettos existed, King had to find a clear issue before he could move in to expose the truth.

Benjamin Willis, the superintendent of schools, gave King the perfect opportunity to prove his point. Willis had become a symbol of Northern segregation because he refused to integrate Chicago's schools. When predominantly black schools become overcrowded, he leased trailers for black students rather than allow them into the same classrooms with whites. King planned to organize a march through Chicago in protest.

Mayor Daley was always a master politician. No sooner did he hear of King's plans to march into Chicago than he released Willis from his duties. Temporarily, King was stopped in his tracks. But quickly regrouping, he focused on another issue, a campaign to end slums.

Open housing was a major issue in every urban area. While there were no signs or laws preventing blacks from living wherever they chose, in reality they were restricted to areas or ghettos where they lived in inferior housing. They paid high rents for rat-infested houses, sometimes without heat or hot water.

Just as King was about to announce his new campaign, Mayor Daley, who had previously denied that there were any ghettos in his city, reversed his stand and announced a major effort to eradicate slums by 1967. Again King found himself outfoxed. He had never encountered anyone like Mayor Daley. The Northern version of segregation was far more subtle than anything in the South. But there was another major difference. In the South, the black ministers were the major tool for organizing the people. Each minister controlled his own congregation and King's base was within those institutions. When a minister asked his congregation to join him in a demonstration, they followed automatically.

In Chicago, the problem of getting the local ministers together to support King was much more complex. Many of the black ministers were in collaboration with the mayor, whose powerful organization could easily crush opposition. His machinery could also make it possible to get a church modernized or zoning laws changed. He arranged to get jobs for members of the congregations in exchange for their support. He was famous for passing out chicken in the black community on election day. Because they understood the mayor's power, many of the black ministers did not wholeheartedly welcome King. Many feared that loss of the mayor's support could destroy their church.

Jackson's role prior to King's arrival was crucial.

He knew they could not count on the local ministers for support automatically, and went to work. Jackson spoke to the ministers individually and directly. He had the ability, even in those early years, to "conjure the honor within a man, that may have been buried inside for years." He appealed to their morality, their humanity, and their manhood. During the weeks before King's arrival, he approached local ministers with pleas, arguments, and challenges to stand up to injustice, and finally won over a great many of them. When King arrived in Chicago in July 1966, Jackson, with a large group of other ministers, was there to meet him.

The credit for organizing King's first major rally belonged mainly to Jackson for getting people to respond in a city that had been complacent for a very long time—where the people believed that nothing could ever be done to improve their condition in life. Sixty thousand people attended the rally to hear Dr. King speak. King appreciated Jackson's major contribution to his first serious effort in Chicago, a city that Jackson understood more intimately than did King.

King called for open housing, nondiscriminatory mortgages, and citizen groups to be established to investigate a series of alleged police brutalities.

The mayor jumped the gun with each issue. He promised King that all those problems would be handled head on. He made public announcements concerning housing and fair mortgage practices. Initially it seemed that King and his followers had pushed the ever-powerful mayor to major concessions, and the public applauded King's accomplishments. It looked as if significant improvements were being made to improve the lives of people in the ghettos. But the efforts were futile.

The programs the mayor had promised never came to pass. Then in 1967 the mayor won re-election by a landslide, capturing 73 percent of the votes. This further embarrassed King and his group. If things were so bad in the ghettos, how could the mayor continue winning? Daley could claim joyfully, "How bad can conditions be, if the community votes for you in great majority?"

King left Chicago disappointed. His efforts had failed. He was not accustomed to dealing with a politician like Daley. He didn't know how to get results from him. A man of principle, King was appalled that anyone of the mayor's stature would renege on his promises so blatantly. He assumed that he would follow through with his commitments. But Daley used every opportunity to his advantage, and unkept promises were not new to his style.

OPERATION BOYCOTT

When King returned to the South, he left Jackson behind to run Operation Breadbasket, the economic arm of the SCLC. The only other full-time staff member of Operation Breadbasket was David Wallace, a white Texan who was Jackson's schoolmate at Chicago Seminary. "Dr. King named the program Operation Breadbasket because its goal was to bring bread, money, and income into the baskets of black and poor people," said Dr. Abernathy.

In Chicago, civil rights leaders had learned early on that marches and sit-ins were not the answer to the problems of discrimination. Economic boycotts or "selective purchasing" produced results. Money was the weapon, and Jackson used that weapon against supermarkets and major companies. His style of protest started a new approach to solving the problems. Somewhat like Robin Hood, he would threaten to boycott a business if his demands were not met. Depending on the specific company, his demands ranged from hiring a number of blacks, to doing business with

Standing on the balcony of the Lorraine Motel
in Memphis, Tennessee, on April 3, 1968,
are, from left to right, Hosea Williams,
Jesse Jackson, Rev. Martin Luther King,
Jr., and Rev. Ralph Abernathy.

companies owned by blacks, to training blacks in management positions. If the companies did not comply, Jackson's followers would, by boycotting them, hurt them where it seemed to count the most—in the pocketbook.

Not only was this approach different from sit-ins and marches, but the notion that a business in the black community should hire blacks, that large companies like Coca-Cola should consider offering people in their own communities the opportunity to buy franchises, that a store should hire a black company to exterminate the roaches, were new ways of looking at the problem. He took the idea of segregation and integration to another level. He demanded that blacks be integrated into the economic structure, and that educated black consumers develop new power—their buying power. It seemed like a simple idea, but consumers needed to understand that it was their purchasing power that made the difference.

Jackson was an early advocate of "black capitalism," working within the existing economic system rather than talking about destroying it, as some other more radical leaders had advocated.

In a relatively short time, his efforts produced results. His threats of boycotts became enough for some businesses to start negotiating and make changes in their business practices. The demands were relatively simple. He wanted the hiring of more blacks, the training and elevating of blacks into higher positions, and the hiring of black contractors—in short, economic gains for black people.

The philosophy was straightforward. "Don't give our people what they need and all the blacks will stop using your products," said Operation Breadbasket.

As Jackson put it, "We are the margin of profit of every major item produced in America, from General Motors on down to Kellogg's Corn Flakes," and "Black banks are to the economic system what blood is to the human system."

33

Jackson and Operation Breadbasket organized the local ministers and decided on a target business in their neighborhood. They researched the business. They investigated the number of blacks working there, and in what capacity, or how many black products the company was using. Then they drew up their demands and sent them to the company. If a company ignored the demands, the ministers informed their congregations that the business was "off limits" until the demands were met.

Country Delight, a dairy business, was the first target of the economic boycott. This company was selected because it employed no black milk drivers or salespeople in jobs that paid more than $12,000 a year. When Jackson approached the managers in the summer of 1966, they refused to disclose their records. The following Sunday, the call went out to all the black churches: "Do not do business with Country Delight." It took only three days to feel the power of the black consumer. Dairy products spoil quickly so their loss was immediately felt. The company responded by offering new jobs to nearly fifty blacks and upgrading other positions.

This first test was a major success and a tremendous psychological victory for Operation Breadbasket and the members of the black community. They began to feel that if they could use their power so effectively, taking action that did not cause any major hardship, they would have a greater control over their own lives. For Jackson, it was a clear sign of accomplishment.

The boycott waged against the supermarket chain Red Rooster in 1969 brought a lot of attention. Red Rooster was well known for its large number of health violations. The stores, located in the primarily black South Side of Chicago, sold poor-quality meat that was already spoiled. Operation Breadbasket brought attention to these practices and demanded not only that the chain hire blacks, but that it clean up its stores. Red Rooster's manager called Jackson a liar and an opportunist. To that charge, Jackson responded, "Yes, I am an opportunist for justice—because I seize every opportunity to try to right a wrong, whether it's in schools, stores, or anywhere black people are being disrespected." The boycott against Red Rooster was a major success. The entire chain went out of business.

Operation Breadbasket achieved national exposure with the lengthy boycott against A & P, which owned a large number of stores in black neighborhoods. The victory here was significant. Operation Breadbasket claimed to have caused A&P to lose $10 million in sales. Although the company held out for some time, it finally agreed to hire over two hundred blacks. When the company balked at training blacks for executive positions, Jackson replied, "If the Army can teach a Negro to build bridges in Vietnam after a six-month training program, a company doesn't need two years to teach him to sell a soda pop successfully."

A & P also agreed to stock black products on store shelves and display them prominently. Furthermore, the company agreed to use black services, such as garbage collection, pest control, and janitorial needs. As Jackson put it, "We have a monopoly on rats in the ghetto and we're going to have a monopoly on killing them." By the time A & P settled with Operation Breadbasket, the company had lost over $10 million. It was the most successful victory the operation had achieved over any supermarket chain.

As the economic boycotts became more successful, Jackson opened up other economic fronts. He pressed for all businesses to invest in black banks, to create a spiral effect. If the black businesses were doing well, they in turn could support some of the needs of the black community more effectively by

Jesse Jackson gives the clenched-fist salute
from a police van after he and eleven others
from Operation Breadbasket were arrested
following a sit-in at the A & P executive
offices in New York City in February 1971.

offering mortgages and lending greater amounts of money to new black businesses or offering students financial aid. All this would vitalize the economy.

The most important premise was the notion that black people were not powerless. Their economic power could be used to work for them. Previously, many black people had believed that because they had so little money to spend, what they did spend did not make a difference to a multimillion-dollar company. Because of the success of the boycotts, they became aware that they did have power and could collectively make a significant difference.

Jackson extended Operation Breadbasket to other cities, but these efforts were not as successful. In Chicago, Jackson worked closely with local preachers, who passed the word along to the community. When he went to other cities the same tight-knit organization was missing, making those boycotts less and less powerful.

SATURDAY-MORNING
MEETINGS

By 1967 Jackson had his own pulpit. In an old auditorium in Chicago's South Side, Jackson began speaking Saturday mornings on a regular basis. These Saturday-morning meetings became Jackson's power base. During the week he traveled around the country, giving speeches, but on Saturday he was back in Chicago to conduct a combination of religious service, strategy meeting, and social gathering. One woman who lived in Chicago recalled, "Everybody went. For one reason or another, it was the place to be. Some went to get spiritual uplifting, others went to take part in the boycotts, or just wanted to see a friend. Some Saturdays the place was so jammed you'd have to get there early or you didn't get a seat."

The sermons, or "preachings," were broadcast on radio, thereby spreading the word and increasing Jackson's exposure in the community. From these revival meetings emerged the now famous expression, "I am somebody."

The combination of Jackson's talent as a preacher, his ability to reach the emotions of his people, along with his ability to offer concrete solutions to their problems, made him a unique leader. He continued to be a Southern Baptist preacher while looking as if he had just stepped out of a ghetto, wearing blue jeans, boots, and a large Afro. At the same time, he was familiar with the profits and losses of corporations, and gave lessons in economics to his adoring audience. Jackson built his base in Chicago. The Saturday-morning sermons were an integral part of building his following.

Many saw him as a new type of leader. He was appealing to the young, who viewed him as a doer with little time to waste. Unlike more traditional preachers who held out the promise of a better life in the hereafter, he demanded better conditions for poor blacks while they were living, insisting that they did not have to settle for less.

Some people were critical of Operation Breadbasket. They disliked Jackson's approach, calling his style "extortion" from white-owned businesses. Others questioned the actual gains made through this approach. They argued that those gains were not monitored, and many companies made promises they never fulfilled. Undoubtedly, as time went by, it was hard to continue pressuring businesses, and Operation Breadbasket did not have the staff to see that businesses honored their commitments.

Others argued that the only black businesses that made gains were those friendly with Jackson.

However, few disagree that Jackson and Operation Breadbasket made a major impact on the lives of the people of Chicago: more blacks were hired, the use of black services by white businesses was increased, and, clearly, economic boycotts were proven to be an effective weapon against racist businesses and a viable tool for nonviolent protests.

3
PUSH

By 1970, two years after the death of Martin Luther King, Jr., Jesse Jackson was a well-known leader in SCLC. He was on the cover of *Time* magazine at twenty-seven, among the youngest of a handful of blacks ever to achieve that honor. These years were notable for some acknowledged victories, including the economic boycotts and the growth of his following influenced by his Saturday-morning "sermons."

Jackson was a great "idea" person. What distinguished him from some of the other civil rights leaders was his sense of the people. He knew that they might be willing to suffer to participate in a protest, but he found a way to make protesting fun and relatively painless. Since the boycotts were not unlawful, none of the protesters were arrested. Nor was undue hardship placed on them—if they boycotted one store chain, they could buy their milk from another.

BLACK EXPO

Consistent with his economic thrust, as early as 1969 he introduced another novel plan—Black Expo, a convention of business people and merchants to exchange ideas and stimulate black business. Because Jackson was well liked in the entertainment industry, he was able to ask some of the best-known black talent to provide entertainment. Attendance at Black Expo was high. Black and white business people came from all over the country, business contacts were established, and small minority businesses found new outlets for their products and services. People also came to hear famous entertainers and just have fun. For Jackson, the center of attention, it was a great success. It was his "baby" and not a SCLC program. He established himself with the public as his own man.

THE BREAK WITH SCLC

The break from SCLC was inevitable and only a matter of time. Since the death of King, friction between Jackson and other leaders of SCLC had been growing, and the relationship between Jackson and Dr. Abernathy, who had been King's closest associate, became strained. Jackson essentially functioned as an autonomous unit in Chicago, gaining publicity and building his own power base. He often ignored Abernathy, running Operation Breadbasket as he saw fit.

The first Black Expo had been staged under the banner of SCLC in conjunction with Operation Breadbasket. All proceeds for the trade show went to SCLC. The following year, Operation Breadbasket staged

In a rare moment of friendly banter, Jesse Jackson explains a "black power handshake" to Chicago's Mayor Richard Daley at the opening of the 1971 Black Expo.

another Black Expo, but this time the organizers incorporated themselves under the name "Black Expo," allegedly without the knowledge or permission of SCLC. This meant that SCLC would not receive proceeds from the event. Jackson and his team claimed that they incorporated the event as a separate entity to protect themselves in case they were sued. Abernathy felt that he should have been informed. Jackson claimed that he had been informed in a memo—not the customary way that Jackson communicated.

The auditorium at the 1970 Black Expo was decorated with huge photographs of Jackson, King, and the then president of the National Urban League, Whitney Young, but there was no photograph of Abernathy, even though he was the president of SCLC.

By the time the convention ended, SCLC and Abernathy were furious. Abernathy felt that the entire event was an affront and an embarrassment to him. He demanded an investigation of the finances of Black Expo. Jackson submitted a report, but Abernathy was not satisfied and suspended him.

PEOPLE UNITED
TO SAVE HUMANITY

The rift with Abernathy may have convinced Jackson that it was time to separate from SCLC. Some people

Jesse Jackson leaves an SCLC executive committee meeting in December 1971, after having been ordered to take a sixty-day leave of absence with pay for what was termed "repeated organizational improprieties."

have suggested that Jackson may have actually staged the confrontation to make it easier to split from SCLC. Having built his own organization by this time, he had nothing to lose. Clearly, he wanted to be on his own. When he left, he took with him his staff and many members of the board of directors of Operation Breadbasket, which did not endear him to SCLC leadership, many of whom had not trusted him since King's death.

Jackson had a flair for the dramatic. As Christmas of 1971 came near, he announced his plans for a new organization. According to some reports, three thousand people went to Chicago's South Side to listen to the announcement of a birth. Speaking from a stage with a huge portrait of Dr. King behind him, he announced that on Christmas Day of 1971, Operation PUSH (People United to Save Humanity) would be officially born. In the words of its founder, it was a "rainbow coalition of blacks and whites gathered together to push for a greater share of economic and political power for all poor people in America in the spirit of Dr. Martin Luther King, Jr."

The goal of PUSH was similar to Operation Breadbasket, the stress being on economic growth. Jackson outlined its purpose: "The goal of our movement at this point in history is to secure jobs for those not working, to get the unemployed employed, and to get those working but not making a livable wage organized. That has to be the thrust of our Civil Economics Movement." He was calling it a "civil economics movement," not a civil rights movement, reflecting the emphasis that he had always placed on economic power—to use money as a means to solve the problems of injustice and discrimination. "We must train our people to use money as a weapon. We've got to be prepared to fight a long time. The Montgomery bus boycott in 1955 lasted a year," Jackson announced.

But PUSH also got involved in the political process—backing candidates, collecting signatures, and registering people to vote.

PUSH EXCEL

In 1975 Jackson turned his attention to the young people. Under a program called "PUSH for Excellence," he began crisscrossing the country to talk to teenagers.

"Our schools are infested with a steady diet of vandalism, violence, drugs, intercourse without discourse, alcohol and TV addiction," he declared.

Traveling to schools and churches around the country, he delivered his message to hundreds of thousands of students. He saw a general attitude of hopelessness. He addressed those teenagers who were coming into adulthood unprepared for the future and without the skills to be productive, employable citizens.

PUSH for Excellence, or "PUSH EXCEL" as the program was later termed, was a reaction to the "loose" morals of America. PUSH EXCEL, like most of Jackson's programs, was based on a simple concept—a respect for traditional values.

As Jackson saw it, youth was floundering in a world without parental leadership, lacking the discipline necessary for success. His message to parents was straightforward: "Only by establishing moral authority, our believability, our trust and worthiness, and our caring, can we demand discipline and have it perceived as therapy and not punishment."

Jackson insisted that parents become involved with their children's education. He encouraged parents to meet their children's teachers, exchange phone numbers with the teachers and with other parents, and to pick up their children's report cards as well as their test scores. He strongly suggested that parents turn off the television set and radio for at least two hours every evening, so that their children could study. There was nothing out of the ordinary in these suggestions. They were simply small steps toward re-establishing parental authority and the bond between parent and teacher.

Jackson's relationship with young people has been most unusual. They have listened to and watched him as if he were their favorite rock star, nodding their heads as he speaks. When he stands up to speak, his young audience is perfectly quiet. He initially demands that everyone remove his hat. Once, after he had finished speaking, a young man came up to talk to him, wearing a wide-brimmed "superfly" hat. He objected to Jackson's demand. He said that he didn't think it made any difference what lay on his head. The important thing was what was inside his head. Jackson listened and nodded, and then explained that while that might be true, if he were to go on a job interview and did not remove his hat, no one would bother to find out what lay inside his skull. The student understood and quietly removed his hat.

His message often has been blunt, venturing into intimate areas avoided by other leaders. In front of a group of high school students, he might say, "Brothers, you're not a man because you can kill somebody. You're not a man because you can make a baby. They can make babies through artificial insemination. Imbeciles can make babies. Fools can make babies. You're a man only if you can raise a baby, protect a baby and provide for a baby." Then they would giggle and laugh, as tension grew in the room. The girls would smile as he addressed the "men" in the audience. But no sooner would they get comfortable than he would turn to them. "There's another side to it, sisters. If you are to deserve the kind of man you cheer for, you cannot spend more time in school on the cultivation of your bosom than your books. If you are to be the right kind of woman, you cannot have a fully developed bottom and a half-developed brain. A donkey got an ass, but he ain't got no sense." They would laugh, cheer, and yell, "Right on."

As one journalist who saw him deliver many speeches noted, "It is this mixture of hipness and traditional, old-fashioned common sense that works so effectively for Jackson when he speaks to students." He hasn't used big words or talked in abstracts. He has been the father figure that many of them never had, with a message that they could understand. He has also placed some of the responsibility of their lives on them. Jackson, himself the father of five children, seems to know and like these students, and this feeling has come across to the audience.

A person ahead of his time, Jackson began addressing the crisis of teenage pregnancy in the mid-seventies, long before America took notice. He talked to both young women and young men, putting the responsibility on both. He hammered away at defining "man" and made them listen to the message that having babies was not a definition of manhood. "I was aware of the odds of survival as a child. I'm still fighting those odds, and defying those odds," he has said repeatedly.

But he also has spoken to them about other things—about the American social system, about hope, dignity, survival, and economic gains through productive jobs. He has stressed the importance of education and striving for excellence. He hasn't hesitated to talk about his own background as an illegitimate child, something with which some students could identify. To them, he has been an example of someone who made it against many odds. He has cited dramatic statistics connecting teenage pregnancy to welfare, despair, and unemployment. They have listened. He has inspired them to feel that they could do what he did and strive for excellence.

The PUSH EXCEL program has had its share of critics. On the one hand, they have felt that Jackson's message has been uplifting for the moment but without lasting influence. There has been no follow-up, no ongoing program and no concrete results. Others suggest that Jackson has placed the burden too heavily on youth, ignoring the complex problems that face them at home, in their neighborhoods, and in their schools. Both arguments have some validity. However, after the program had been in effect for some time, many of the schools noted that absenteeism was sharply reduced. In the Chicago area, the number of knifings and killings dropped on the campuses. At some schools, students started their own clubs, spreading the message of pride.

It is true that Jackson's visits to schools have been short—usually only an hour—but some of the teachers and principals have felt that his message has given them the chance to continue talking about issues that he has raised.

No one knows whether his message has stopped teenagers from becoming pregnant or has influenced them to stay in school, but when he speaks, they listen. Sometimes, a smile, a glitter, comes into those eyes where before there had been a vacant stare. He has left them with a sense of pride, a challenge, and a feeling that they could make it if they really tried.

Jackson has given them a glimmer of hope that can make the difference between resignation and determination. Many of these students had given up, or as he would say, "Their spirit is broken." The odds have seemed against them. It is this feeling that Jackson has tried to change.

Jackson has traveled into hundreds, maybe thousands, of schools across the country, talking, preach-

*Jackson talking with young school children
in New Hampshire in May 1983*

ing, and spreading his message of morality and traditional values. No other leader, black or white, has made these youths such a priority. In return, the students' response has been overwhelming. As one teacher commented, "The students know that you don't quarrel with success." To them, Jackson is the most successful person most of them have ever known or seen.

Beneath the flamboyant style, the fame, and the "hip" and "cool" image of Jackson there seems to be a deeply religious and conservative man. He does not smoke, drink, or take drugs. He works eighteen to twenty hours a day. At times he pushes himself to the point of exhaustion. His concern has been the moral decay of American society. He has said, "Many of us allow our children to eat junk, play with junk, watch junk, listen to junk, and then we're surprised when they come out to be social junkies." He has used slogans and catchy phrases that rhyme. Before leaving the students in an auditorium, he often ends up with his well-known phrase, "I am somebody." As voices in the audience responded to the chant "I am somebody," even reticent students join in, and more and more of the students stand up and shout, "I am somebody," "I may be on welfare . . . but I am somebody," and repeat it. He would go on, "I may be uneducated . . . but I am somebody. I may be hungry, but I am somebody." By now his voice has reached a pitch of ecstasy. And they shout, "I AM SOMEBODY," and with thunderous applause he exits, preaching, "Say it loud, I am somebody."

Some of the students leave the room chanting and quoting him: "You may be in the slum, but the slum doesn't have to be in you. The empire is in your brains. Freedom ain't free. It's not the altitude that determines how high you fly, it's your ATTITUDE."

4

Chicago Years

During the 1960s and 1970s, a common street slogan of the ghettos was "Burn, baby, burn," a cry for a more radical solution to the blacks' condition. But the message that Jackson delivered was different. While some people talked about burning down cities and destroying the system that promoted racism and discrimination, Jackson promoted black pride wherever he spoke. He urged young people to "Learn, baby, learn," rather than "Burn, baby, burn."

Harry Reasoner, an ABC-TV commentator, in October 1973 said, "Jackson makes sure the temperature never gets out of control, and he is not a racist. Jackson wants a share of power without destroying its base, which is good news for blacks, as well as for whites."

Jackson was known for flowery patterns of preaching common to Baptist ministers. Words that sounded like poetry still drove the point across. His phrases had a flowing rhythm, phrases that people could chant, that were remembered long after they were heard.

BLACK PRIDE

In educating black people about the power of using their money wisely, during his Saturday-morning sermons he would say, "You will show your blackness by buying Grove Fresh Orange Juice. Say it loud, 'I am black and I'm proud and I'll buy Grove Fresh Orange Juice.' " Or he would say, "Now Joe Louis milk does not come from a Negro cow. That milk is just like any other milk. It's written right here on the carton. Only difference is that your husband can make twelve thousand dollars a year driving a truck for this company." (In 1970, $12,000 a year was a good salary for a truck driver.)

During that period many black people, including Jackson, wore large Afros as a sign of black pride. But often he would say, "A new hair style does not constitute black power, a new life style does. About the only thing that can save us, is waking up one morning with self-respect."

Aside from delivering numerous speeches filled with messages of pride and respect, he is also a man of ideas. Some people have argued that he has too many ideas to do justice to all the different challenges he takes on at the same time.

BLACK CHRISTMAS

While hospitalized for several days in 1968 because of sickle cell anemia, a blood disease primarily confined to black people of African descent, Jackson was busy exploring new and novel ideas to further black economic development. During this time, one of the leaders of CORE (the Congress of Racial Equality), urged blacks to boycott the Christmas season. Jackson, a pragmatist, sensing that Christmas was too much a tradition to boycott, suggested an alternative, "Black Christmas." Held in Chicago's amphitheater, Black Christmas had one of the best guarantees of success. It was fun. The black business community set up sales counters, hired high school bands, and created colorful floats. Also present was a Black Soul Saint, dressed in a black dashiki, traditional African garb then worn by many blacks. The Black Soul Saint was not the customary Santa Claus who brought presents or material gifts. Instead he offered love, justice, peace, and power.

Everyone was satisfied. Black businesses made money, the ministers were pleased that the spirit of Christmas was promoted, and black middle-class families, encouraged to do so, invited poorer families for Christmas. All these ideas were consistent with the concept of Christmas. Even though Jackson had not introduced this idea until the first week of December, Black Christmas was such a success, he went on to do a similar event for Black Easter the following year and later developed the concept for Black Expo.

Black pride, boycotts, buying from black companies, Black Expos, and Black Christmas were all based on a common goal—the achievement of black economic well-being.

By 1974 Chicago had the largest and strongest financial base of any black community, including eleven black-owned financial institutions. In the 1974 *Black Enterprise* report of the one hundred black-owned firms whose sales volume exceeded $1 million, Chicago with eighteen businesses ranked second to New York. Many of these businesses openly acknowledged that Jackson's influence made the difference. He created an environment that encouraged the community's support of black enterprise. In turn, he asked that the black businesses return some of their wealth to the community. One company set up a

million-dollar scholarship fund, while other businesses sent people food or provided shelter or college tui-
tion. Jackson's economic program was a success.

RUNNING FOR OFFICE

Jackson's first foray into the political arena was in
1971. In a manner that some people consider customary for Jackson, he did not seriously discuss with other black leaders his decision to run against Chicago's
powerful Mayor Richard Daley—a master politician
and the head of a strong political machine.

Expectedly, Jackson lost by many votes. Some
people wondered why he had chosen to run against
such a powerful incumbent. Many politicians opposed
to Daley felt that Jackson was the wrong candidate
and had run a disorganized campaign. Why did he do
it? Perhaps he was intrigued by the idea that anyone
would dare to run against someone like Daley. Until
Jackson, no black had dared to take on the candidacy.
Jackson was known to be courageous, but this time his
boldness seemed a misjudgment.

THE 1972 DEMOCRATIC
CONVENTION

In 1971 Jackson made news again with a higher goal.
He wished to organize a "Liberation party," composed
of black and white liberals, with the clear purpose of
nominating a black for president. His announcement,
however, was not taken seriously. While he and other
black male political leaders floundered in looking for
a candidate, Shirley Chisholm, a black New York
Democratic Congresswoman, announced her candidacy with the Democratic party. She was the first black
woman ever to take on this challenge. Jackson was

stopped. Congresswoman Chisholm was not the Liberation party's candidate, but he certainly would not run a third-party candidate against this well-known Democrat. As one reporter put it, "The year of black unity missed its mark in 1972."

Yet Jackson did manage to win a major political victory. With shrewdness and good timing, he outwitted the master politician Daley, and unseated his delegates to the Democratic Convention.

The party rules stated that delegates must be selected at open meetings and not secretly slated. The rules explicitly forbade the use of party money and resources for its favorite candidates, and the party had to assure fair representation of minorities as delegates in proportion to their presence in the population. Daley liked to control his delegates, something he could not do if they were selected in a truly democratic fashion. "The hell with the rules," he arrogantly proclaimed. The selection was held in secret and the slate was not balanced in representing Illinois's population.

Revealing to the Democratic National Convention Credentials Commission the extent of Daley's violations of party rules, Jackson managed to unseat Mayor Daley's delegates. An open election in Chicago followed and a new slate of delegates was elected. But after this election, Jackson surprisingly offered to compromise with Daley and to share seats. Each delegation would have half a vote in exchange for reforms that would benefit Chicago's black community, such as a civilian police review board.

Many of Jackson's supporters were stunned by this offer. One reporter noted, "Jesse Jackson has a lot of people bothered about his role in trying to be the compromiser in the Illinois credentials fight. He's accused of running with the hares and hunting with the hounds."

But Jackson, now an astute politician, knew what

was at stake. If Daley were ousted, he might not lend his support to the Democratic candidate, George McGovern. Jackson stated, "Given the choice between crushing Daley and elevating McGovern, I would elevate McGovern. We cannot major in a mayor and minor in a president. Being anti-Daley is not the same thing as being pro-black. I am not as committed to destroying the mayor as he has been to [destroying] us. Knocking down the mayor may be necessary, but the major thing is electing a Democratic president against Richard Nixon. The new guard and the old guard of the Democratic party can either live together like people or die apart like fools."

In the presidential election that followed, George McGovern, the Democratic candidate for president, lost badly to the Republican candidate, Richard Nixon. To add insult to injury, not only was the idea for a third-party presidential candidate buried, but after Jackson gave his reluctant support to the Democratic party's George McGovern, he was quickly snubbed by the candidate.

"When McGovern needed black support, he called twice from Wisconsin, came to Operation PUSH, and personally encouraged me to speak for him in the primaries. Since he won [the primaries] I've seen and heard less and less of him . . . I have not changed, McGovern has changed," Jackson later recalled.

A decade later, when Jackson himself ran for the presidency, these events in the past added to his knowledge and ability and were used in waging a historic campaign.

THE OLD ORDER PASSES

Battling with Mayor Daley, a seasoned politician who could deliver the votes to get his people elected, gave

Jackson the opportunity to learn from a tough rival. In calling for a black presidential candidate, he set the stage for entering the mainstream of national politics. He took part in Chicago politics with some gains and some losses. It was a place where he could learn how the political process worked. And by organizing voter-registration drives, he galvanized people into concern for specific issues.

Mayor Daley, who had always seemed unbeatable, died in 1976. His death marked the end of a strong political machine. Chicago, a city of sharp ethnic divisions and segregated housing, began to change. Then Jane Byrne, a white, was elected mayor.

In Chicago's 1983 primary, two white candidates, Jane Byrne and Richard Daley, Jr., and a black candidate, Harold Washington, ran for mayor on the Democratic ticket. In one of the most volatile campaigns ever waged, Washington won the primary and then went on to win the general election in 1984, defeating the Republican, Bernard Epton. While some people questioned Jackson's impact on this election, he undoubtedly helped create the climate that made it possible. He encouraged black people to register in large numbers and campaigned vigorously for Harold Washington. The nation watched this event with enormous interest. If a black man could be elected mayor in Chicago, then it could happen in other major cities in the country.

Jackson always promoted the concept that the black margin made a significant difference and urged the unregistered to vote. For Washington, registering the minorities became an important mission. His victory was proof that black voters made a difference, that they could help determine who would be the next mayor. He campaigned for this cause, educating people about their power, and instilling in them the notion that they were "somebody," that they made a difference, that their votes counted.

Soon after Harold Washington's victory in Chicago in 1984, a black mayor was elected in another large city—Wilson Goode in Philadelphia. The concept was working: minority candidates were running for offices throughout the country and were setting the stage for the top spot, a black presidential candidate.

Jackson, campaigning in Mississippi in 1983, urges young people to register to vote.

5
Run, Jesse, Run

"We picked their cotton. We cooked their food. We nursed their babies. Now, we can run their cities. We can run their states. We will run the country." And in response, the crowd shouted back, "Run, Jesse, Run."

In November 1983, at the Convention Center in Washington, D. C., Jesse L. Jackson made it official. He would seek the Democratic party's nomination for president of the United States.

His bid for the nomination was marked by controversy, excitement, and jealousy. It was a significant moment in American history. It almost didn't matter if he won or lost. His candidacy—the mounting of a major national campaign—was a victory in itself. As he often told his listeners, "If you run, you might lose. But if you don't run, you're guaranteed to lose."

Jackson saw his candidacy as one that would reach a wider scope than only black Americans. It would be a progressive "Rainbow Coalition" of the elderly, of the white Appalachian poor, of Hispanics, Asians, nuclear freeze activists, Third World people, disgruntled farmers, women, and all others ignored by both major parties. As he envisioned it, together they would claim the progressive wing of the Democratic party and become a significant third force outside the two-party system, exerting pressure on both parties. Barbara Reynolds, a journalist who watched Jackson's leadership grow, noted, "He has grown from the black leader, who presided over one of the nation's most premier grass roots civil rights organizations, Operation PUSH, to a universal spokesman for human rights, world peace and international economic justice for developing nations of the Third World."

He was now welcomed by Pope John Paul II, Fidel Castro, the Cuban head of state, and many other leaders around the world. Perhaps no other black leader had received such worldwide attention.

With virtually no television ads, and campaign expenditures of $6.4 million as compared with Mondale's $24.9 million and Gary Hart's $13.9 million, Jackson won 3.5 million votes in the primaries. It is estimated that the campaign, plus his aggressive voter-registration drives across the country, brought in one million new voters. But his campaign could not be measured by votes alone. His candidacy initiated a mass movement, bringing thousands of people into

A little boy at a 1984 Democratic primary campaign rally in the Watts section of Los Angeles holds up a picture of Jesse Jackson. Jackson, speaking before an audience of about two thousand people, said, "Hart and Mondale mean well, but they don't understand what it is like to be poor."

"Our Time Has Come"

the political process who had never participated in the system before. A new generation of workers learned to work in a national campaign, while hundreds of other black candidates ran for lesser offices, and many won.

Jackson often has pointed out, "My race was never about running for the White House alone. It was about ten thousand people running in their states for the school board, and sheriffs and state legislatures, for congress, mayor and governor."

THE "IMPERFECT SERVANT"

But Jackson's campaign had as many adversaries in the black community as in the white. Many of the most prominent Democratic black officials viewed his candidacy negatively. They felt that Jackson might hurt the chances of Democratic front-runner Walter Mondale against the Republican presidential candidate, Ronald Reagan. Prominent leaders, such as Mayor Coleman Young of Detroit, Mayor Andrew Young of Atlanta, Mayor Tom Bradley of Los Angeles, Benjamin Hooks of the NAACP, and even Coretta King, Dr. King's widow, did not support his bid for president. They felt that it was more important to the black community to defeat Ronald Reagan than to run a black candidate. Others argued that Jackson had never held an elected office, had never run a national campaign, and as an outsider to the political process, was ill equipped to run a campaign on a major national scope. Owing to a lack of funds, his campaign was disorganized and weak.

It was believed that Mondale would have a hard time beating Ronald Reagan, the presidential incumbent, but Jackson in the race would hurt Mondale's chances further by siphoning off the black vote. This, in fact, proved to be an accurate assessment. In the

1984 Democratic primaries, Jackson managed to win high percentages of black votes—79 percent in Illinois and 87 percent in New York. Nationwide he captured 10 percent of the nonblack vote. A leading black magazine *Jet* boldly stated, "By now critics have been forced to concede that the candidacy of Reverend Jesse Jackson for United States President has been nothing short of brilliant. Running what he calls a 'poor campaign with a rich message,' he's proven that a black man can run for President in America."

Jackson was greatly criticized by the Jewish community. While he supported Israel's right to exist, he also endorsed the idea that the Palestinian people had a right to their homeland, some of which was occupied by Israel. In this very controversial issue among Jews, Jackson took what was considered to be an anti-Israeli position. His public stance of friendship with Palestine Liberation Organization (PLO) leader Yasser Arafat was offensive to many Jews and non-Jews alike who considered Arafat an enemy of Israel and a dangerous terrorist.

On another score, Jackson criticized the United States foreign-aid policy. He argued that while Africa was receiving less than $300 million in U.S. foreign aid for 530 million people, Israel, with 4 million people, was receiving $2 billion. Some of Israel's supporters quickly pointed out that the United States had to support Israel because it is the main ally in the Middle East, situated near hostile neighbors.

To make matters worse, Jackson was quoted as minimizing the suffering of Jews. In a statement that Jackson claims was taken out of context, he said, "I am sick and tired of hearing about the Holocaust and having America put in a position of a guilt trip . . . Jewish people do not have a monopoly on suffering."

There were many threats on Jackson's life— according to him, over three hundred. Some of his campaign offices were fire-bombed. The militant

Jewish Defense League threatened to picket Jackson's home, and placed ads in newspapers asking for contributions to stop Jackson's campaign.

Then, just as his campaign was gaining strength with controversy and a great deal of excitement, the *New York Times* reported shortly before the New York primary, "In private conversation with reporters, Jackson referred to Jews as 'Hymies' and to New York as 'Hymietown.'" "Hymie" is considered a derogatory term for Jews. At first, Jackson denied that he made the comment, then stated that he couldn't remember if he had. After weeks of pressure from the press, he admitted that he had made it. However, he claimed to have been unaware that the comment was offensive to Jews. As he recalled the incident, the remark had been made in a casual off-record conversation with several black reporters, including Milton Coleman. Unexpectedly, Coleman mentioned it in his article in the *Washington Post*, and the uneasy relationship between Jackson and the Jewish community worsened. Some of his liberal white supporters felt that they could no longer back him, while others felt that the incident was greatly exaggerated and blown out of proportion. The dark clouds lingered for some time. One of Jackson's followers and main supporters, Louis Farrakhan, a prominent Black Muslim leader, further exacerbated the situation. In one statement, made by Farrakhan on March 11, 1984, he seemed to threaten the life of the reporter for exposing the incident. Because the Black Muslim minister played a role in the Jackson campaign, and his "Fruits of Islam" served as bodyguards for the candidate, Farrakhan's statement added fuel to the fire and cast a shadow over Jackson's campaign.

Finally, after several weeks of extreme pressure, Jackson, in a statement to the press, disassociated himself from Farrakhan's statements, but quickly pointed out that it was unfair of the media to hold him accountable for another person's behavior. The Farrakhan controversy dimmed some of Jackson's victories of the campaign, for example, Jackson's receiving in the Democratic primary 21 percent of the votes in Georgia and 19 percent in Alabama. Reporters would not leave the issue alone. Later on, Jackson, addressing the Democratic Convention in San Francisco, publicly apologized.

"If in my low moments, in word, deed, or attitude, through some error of temper, taste, or tone, I have caused anyone discomfort, created pain, or revived someone's fears, that was not my truest self, please forgive me. Charge it to my head, so limited in its finitude, not to my heart, which is boundless in its love for the entire human family. I am not a perfect servant, I am a public servant, doing my best as I develop and serve against the odds. Be patient. God is not finished with me yet."

THE RAINBOW COALITION

Many felt that Jackson's speech showed grace and maturity. In the same speech, he reminded America of its true rainbow colors: blacks, American Indians, women, whites, Jews, the disabled, Hispanics, the elderly, displaced farmers, and children. "America rejects and excludes more people than it accepts and includes," said Jackson. "The Rainbow Coalition easily constitutes the new majority."

Though Jackson lost the Democratic party's nomination, he won 384 delegates, more than had been predicted. Certainly his platform made an impact, and his agenda was an influence on the party's platform.

The Rainbow Coalition was described as "an attempt to organize the political strength of all deprived and rejected constituencies around the moral force and political energy of the black movement . . . the civil rights movement that built the foundations, provided the climate and in many instances, the initial organizers." The coalition's platform advocated strong enforcement of the Voting Rights Act, affirmative action, and "equality of opportunity and participation in all aspects of our economic, social and political life for the historic victims of discrimination."

It supported the Equal Rights Amendment (ERA), guaranteeing equal rights to women under the Constitution. The coalition also supported the right of women to choose to have an abortion, otherwise known as "Pro Choice." The rainbow platform opposed restrictions on federal funding for abortion, stating that because the poor were unable to pay for abortions, by eliminating federal funding they would be discriminated against.

The platform called for support and expanded rights for the disabled; elimination of discrimination based on sexual preference, or "Gay Rights"; the right of Native Americans to have greater control of their land without interference from the Bureau of Indian Affairs, a government agency that monitors Indian activities.

In foreign affairs, the platform advocated an immediate nuclear freeze and promoted arms-reduction negotiations with the Soviets. Jackson advocated removing all troops from Central America, opposed aid to the "Contras" of Nicaragua, and suggested support for a Palestinian state. A champion against apartheid, he urged United States corporations to cut off all investments in South Africa. He said, "Apartheid is violence by definition . . . it rules on fears and lies, it violates free will, burns the body, limits the mind."

"When they write the history of this [Democratic primary] the longest chapter will be on Jackson. The man didn't have two cents. He didn't have one television or radio ad. And look at what he did," said Mario Cuomo, the governor of New York. What Jackson did was in many ways not measurable. Close to 20 percent of the convention delegates were black in 1984 compared with 14 percent at the 1980 convention and 10 percent in 1976. This obviously major contribution was directly attributable to his campaign.

He raised issues throughout the campaign that no one else had mentioned. He talked about the disenfranchised people of the United States who felt ignored by the system, and got those people involved and registered to vote. He raised U.S. consciousness simply by being in the limelight every day, hammering away about the problems of the poor and those he described as part of the Rainbow Coalition. He reminded Americans that these problems had to be addressed by a presidential candidate as well. "I want to be respected and heard . . . the issues I raise and the constituency I represent won't go away," he stated. He forced the Democratic party to listen. He forced the nation to take notice.

While the civil rights movement of the 1960s was a major step toward integration, with the Voting Rights Act establishing a more equal society, Jackson's Rainbow Coalition was an idealistic movement that raised issues about all people who felt "locked out" of full participation in this society. His platform focused not only on blacks, but on the elderly, the handicapped, on women, and on other disadvantaged groups. His platform was an alternative; his concerns were for those people who are often considered "underdogs"—the poor, the hungry, and those without power.

Walter Mondale won the nomination as Democratic candidate, but according to the Gallup Poll, Jackson had become the most important black American. His candidacy made history, though his campaign had virtually no money. While five other candidates,

all white, had dropped out of the race for lack of support, Jackson remained in the race until the end.

His presidential campaign was one of hope, with a moving battle cry. "There's a freedom train a coming," he preached. "But you got to be registered to ride. Get on board . . . get on board . . . we can move from the slaveship to the championship, from the guttermost to the uppermost, from the outhouse to the courthouse, from the state house to the White House." And crowds cheered him on: "Oh, yes, oh yes, we will. Run, Jesse, run."

Jesse L. Jackson was indeed somebody, a formidable presence on the American political scene. As one journalist put it, "For that period, the nation was stunned into silence by the vision of something that was beautiful, powerful and even awesome. The black man had finally undeniably arrived on the American scene." That vision of Jackson addressing the Democratic party's convention was a moment that brought many Americans to tears. He was in some ways bigger than life. He seemed to represent the unbroken connection between the people who died in the civil rights movement and the present, a continuation of the struggle of those people who felt that they were underrepresented or locked out of their own country.

Walter Mondale and Jesse Jackson.
When Mondale became the
Democratic party's choice
to run against the Republican
presidential incumbent
Ronald Reagan, Jackson
campaigned hard for Mondale.

6

Jackson's Foreign Affairs Policies

Shortly after Jackson announced his candidacy for president in December 1983, a U.S. Navy fighter/bomber was shot down over Lebanon. The pilot was killed and the navigator/bombardier, Lt. Robert O. Goodman, Jr., a black American, was taken as a "prisoner of war." Jackson believed that the Reagan administration did not negotiate Goodman's release aggressively enough. In an unprecedented move, he decided to "get into the act." Defying the State Department's opposition, in the first month of the new year he engaged in a personal diplomatic mission to free the captured airman.

A FAR JOURNEY

Jackson had already met the Syrian president Hafez al-Assad in 1979, during his tour of the Middle East. They had established a good relationship of mutual respect. Jackson believed that he would have a better chance of success in winning Goodman's release than the United States government. It was a risky move, and even his own staff members were worried. If he did not succeed, he would be criticized from all sides. The State Department and the diplomatic community would have every right to condemn Jackson for personally negotiating with a foreign government. If his mission failed, the government could lose any other chance for further negotiations and the captured American's life might be in jeopardy.

Nevertheless, Jackson, despite serious opposition and great risk, traveled eight thousand miles to Syria and appealed to that government on humanitarian grounds for the American's release. He traveled without any secret-service protection, provided to all presidential candidates, as a gesture of good faith. He thus showed that he trusted the Syrian government to protect his safety. "Whoever has the courage should act," he commented about his trip. He traveled to Syria without the State Department's sanction, knowing that should anything happen to him, he was fully responsible for his own actions. It was his decision.

Initially, it seemed as if his trip would do no more than generate publicity with no concrete results. Four tense days passed before he was granted the opportunity to meet with Syrian President al-Assad. He appealed to him directly. The United States government had failed but Jackson was able to convince President al-Assad that keeping Lieutenant Goodman might escalate the number of U.S. reconnaissance flights over Syrian-held territory. Apparently, al-Assad was impressed by this message. Jackson's efforts yielded results. The twenty-seven-year-old Navy airman was unexpectedly released from a Syrian prison and flown back to the United States with Jackson on an official plane.

They returned to a national hero's welcome. All the cameras were on Jackson, whose mission was a major victory. The White House, unsuccessful at delivering this result, had to acknowledge Jackson's

Jesse Jackson is shown here with
Lt. Robert Goodman in Damascus, Syria,
in December 1983. Shortly afterwards,
Jackson succeeded in gaining Goodman's
release and returned with him to
the United States.

achievement. "Jackson has earned our gratitude and our admiration," was the official White House statement.

In the Rose Garden at the White House, the day was devoted to Lieutenant Goodman, whom many had given up for dead. At Jackson's side, Goodman's parents expressed their gratitude. With extensive press coverage of the event, Jackson's prestige grew. He had proven that he could achieve what the White House had failed to do, the peaceful release of an American airman shot down over foreign soil in the line of duty.

Jackson had also proven himself to be a diplomat and a successful negotiator. His warm relations with the Arab leadership were tested, and had paid off.

His trip to Lebanon was a turning point in his campaign. He received considerable media attention as a person who could handle foreign affairs and sensitive issues concerning a foreign government. He was no longer a black candidate running a symbolic campaign. Some felt that he had demonstrated that he was presidential material. He could act in difficult situations and get results.

MISSION TO CUBA

Jackson's other highly dramatic gesture during the campaign was his trip to Cuba. The United States had been unsuccessful in developing good relations with the government of Cuba and its leader, Fidel Castro. This Soviet-backed nation was accused by the United States of encouraging the spread of communism in Latin America. Because of Cuba's ties to the Soviet Union, there had been no successful attempt to negotiate with Cuba or to develop a relationship of trust. Castro has not been invited to the White House, nor has the president visited Cuba.

In 1984, Jackson took advantage of an opportunity

to meet with the Cuban leader during his campaign. He talked with him for more than eight hours. "There was a lot of common understanding," Jackson reported. "He's in the Third World and I have a Third World experience in suffering and exploitation. We identify with a lot of the same people in Africa and Central America." Jackson was greeted with enthusiasm in Cuba; he is the only presidential candidate to have visited Castro's Cuba and to treat that country as an important entity.

But his trip proved to be more than just symbolic. Unexpectedly, Castro released forty-eight prisoners, twenty-two of whom were Americans. Most of the Americans had spent one to four years in jail, on charges of drug trafficking. For the most part, they were arrested after equipment failures on boats or planes had forced them into Cuban waters.

The twenty-six jailed Cubans had been in prison for more than twenty years. They, unlike their American counterparts, were imprisoned for political offenses against the Castro government. They never expected to leave prison alive.

In "Little Havana," a strongly anti-Castro Cuban-American neighborhood in Miami, many supported Jackson's effort on purely pragmatic grounds. The sentiments of a man who had given Jackson a list of political prisoners in advance of his trip to Havana were mixed: "I will stand up anywhere and tell Jackson publicly, 'Thank you for freeing the prisoners,' but in the next breath I will say I'm disappointed because I don't share Jackson's foreign policy views. Castro has been a dictator for twenty-five years and Jackson is going out there and embracing him and calling him everything short of God."

Jackson's success further demonstrated his ability to negotiate with unfriendly foreign governments. His efforts seemed to indicate that he cared about all people, Cubans as well as Americans.

Jackson often talked passionately about the need

to promote peace on earth. His sentiments are the same today. He says he is willing to talk to any of the world's leaders, regardless of the kind of government they head. He believes that the United States should not ignore Cuba, a neighboring country that has had a communis. government for over twenty years. He believes it is foolish not to try to re-establish normal relations.

AFRICA

In 1986, Jackson traveled to eight African countries in seventeen days, and ABC television network's *20/20* captured the experience on videotape. He traveled through hunger-stricken areas and saw people dying of starvation. Wherever he went, a trail of people cheered him as if a long-lost leader had come home at last. In a symbolic way, he *was* coming home, returning to Africa after some four hundred years, bringing hope and leadership to his motherland. As Jackson prayed on African soil, President Kenneth Kaunda of Zambia stood by in tears. The president of Mozambique, Samora Machel, hugged and kissed him. Later in the year, after Machel was killed in a plane crash, the Mozambique government invited Jackson to head the American delegation to attend President Machel's funeral.

During one of his many press conferences, Jackson focused on the issue of apartheid, the policy of racial separation in South Africa. He stated that American corporations doing business in South Africa were directly contributing to that government's apartheid policy. He said that as long as these corporations and the U.S. government dealt with that country, South Africa would not change this policy. The only way to fight apartheid was to stop doing business with the South African regime supporting it.

Jackson with Zimbabwe Prime
Minister Robert Mugabe, during
Jackson's 1986 African tour

President Samora Machel of Mozambique
meets with Jackson in August 1986.
Later in the year, when Machel was
killed in an airplane accident,
Jackson headed the American
delegation to attend the funeral.

Jackson's well publicized opposition to the South African government reinforced the efforts of students in major universities who were demonstrating against apartheid, demanding that their schools divest themselves of any financial interest in South Africa.

During Jackson's 1986 trip to Africa, he visited many of the countries geographically close to South Africa. An undeclared war wages between the white South African government and these countries. South Africa believes that these countries help black rebel forces fight against the South African government.

As a major critic of the Reagan administration's policy toward South Africa, Jackson urged a summit between leaders of Africa and the administration. At a press conference in New York City in the fall of 1986, he said, "President Reagan should accept the Front Line heads of states' request for a summit meeting to meet their emergency aid requirements. The drought continues in Mozambique and southern Africa; furthermore, we should assist in providing defensive aid against the South African–backed rebels . . . alerting public opinion in our country to the suffering that this has caused was the main purpose of the pilgrimage to the Front Line states [the states surrounding South Africa]." Jackson continued, "We urge all people of good will to intensify the efforts to enforce comprehensive economic sanctions against the apartheid regime by refusing to buy any South African goods."

CENTRAL AMERICA

Concerning the United States policy on Central America, he advocated "contacting your Congress member immediately to urge that all aid to the Contras be stopped." The Contras, Nicaraguan insurgents with sanctuaries in neighboring Honduras, were attempting to overthrow Nicaragua's socialist regime. Congress was vehemently debating whether or not the United States government should be involved in another country's internal affairs by supplying arms to the Contras.

As part of his foreign-affairs policy, Jackson also took a lead in opposing aid to the opposition group. To many, our involvement in Nicaragua was a reminder of how we got involved in Vietnam, and the heavy toll it extracted in lives, morale, and money.

Jackson has advocated a general reduction in arms as well as a nuclear freeze. He has expressed concern about hunger in the United States and the lack of federal funds for farmers, the poor, and the elderly. In his view, the money spent on building arms and on developing more sophisticated weaponry should instead be spent on those in need, the disadvantaged in this country and around the world. He has explained carefully to his audiences that there is a direct connection between producing arms to support the Contras in Nicaragua and the Reagan administration's cutback in social services, such as aid to single mothers and school-lunch programs.

THE GLOBAL VIEW

Jackson has been talking more and more about all people, and less and less only about civil rights for blacks. He has taken part in demonstrations for peace and for jobs. He has addressed the problem of our uneasy relationship with the Soviet Union, urging that greater efforts be made for a successful summit meeting between the two countries. In 1986, speaking in New York before a large gathering of peace marchers, he passionately denounced Reagan's Strategic Defense Initiative (SDI), commonly called Star Wars.

Some of Jackson's critics have regarded his foreign policy as shallow and simplistic. They contend that he does not examine global issues in depth, and that he does not understand the complexities. They maintain that if he had the responsibility of actually establishing policy and carrying it out on a day-to-day basis, he would learn that there are no easy solutions, that there are innumerable problems that require patience and compromise.

But more and more, Jackson has voiced the concerns of liberals and taken a stand alongside leaders of movements concerned with such issues as Nicaragua, women's rights, the homeless, and world peace. He is the only black leader who has joined forces with many different groups in an effort to create an effective "Rainbow Coalition."

7

Jesse L. Jackson, the Man

Barbara Reynolds, a journalist who has traveled extensively with Jackson noted, "He is a man so personable; disliking him would take practice. He is the kind of man that babies instinctually kiss. When he is around, the neighborhood hound who barks at everyone wags his tail." This same reporter recalled his sense of humor. "I lost my notebook," she said. "It was filled with personal gush from his many adversaries. He found it and gave it back. 'Barbara,'" he said, "'I don't know what kind of super-sleuth you're going to be if you keep losing the evidence.'"

Jackson has many health problems: sickle cell anemia, back pains, and repeated bouts with pneumonia. He often works past the point of exhaustion. However, he never complains about his health. His stamina, his persistence, and his positiveness come across.

To gain insight into a "typical day" for Jesse Jackson, in 1986 I spent some time with him and his associates. Traveling with Jesse Jackson was a tiring experience. When he asks, "How are you?", after you have just arrived on a 6:25 A.M. flight from New York to Chicago, you would not think of saying "tired." His daily work schedule took up eighteen to twenty hours. That is not unique for people who are actively campaigning for an elected office, but Jackson always works that way. It is his way of life. Even though he is no longer the head of PUSH, whenever possible, he returns to Chicago for the Saturday-morning meeting.

SATURDAY MORNINGS
AT PUSH

PUSH headquarters is a huge building, with a large auditorium and beautiful stained-glass windows. The building is awesome. It has no graffiti and seems to shine with pride.

The meeting was in session, the Reverend Jesse Jackson presiding. The experience was a unique mixture of prayer, choir singing, gospel music, fund raising, and a touch of a town meeting broadcast live on the radio. The place was filled with people, all kinds of people.

There were young people, old people, well-dressed people, white people and black people, people of different religions, and little children, all mesmerized by Jackson. He was on the podium, revealing his soul to the people. Repeatedly, people spontaneously rose and shouted back, "Preach, preach. Educate us." On this day, he was talking passionately about South Africa and its racist system of apartheid. Interwoven in his talk was a message about getting out to vote in the next local election, a fierce fight between a Democrat and a Republican. If the Republican won, it would be a vote for South Africa; a Democratic victory would mean a vote against South Africa.

He could see everything from the podium, feeling the rhythm of the audience and seeming to know precisely what they were thinking and feeling at that moment. The people were at home with him. There was a real familiarity in the place, as if everyone in the audience was a part of one family with shared problems. There was a warmth reaching out from the stage. Each person felt as if Jackson were talking to him or her alone. The people talked back to him from their seats. As the soulful choir sang, he moved with the rhythm of the beat, clapping his hands, swaying his body, and tapping his feet. During those two hours, the audience felt no pain, only joy, pride, and unity. They were truly his family.

ON THE CAMPAIGN TRAIL

But on a typical day, the ten o'clock sermon was just the beginning of what was to follow. This day was dedicated to campaigning for local Democratic politicians, running for various offices from treasurer to lieutenant governor to secretary of state. We were out campaigning from one end of the city to the other, yet Jackson was not running for anything.

"What makes you do this—for twenty years?" I wanted to know. For a moment I could see his eyes searching for an answer to a question that he must have heard hundreds of times. "It is for my self-respect. I am the subject of pain. I feel the pain." He paused, as if to ask whether I had understood what he had said. He looked pensive, but always aware of his surroundings, appreciating each and every moment to its fullest. He proceeded to tell me a story.

"I was at the Helmsley Palace Hotel in New York to meet President Robert Mugabe of Zimbabwe. I helped this lady bring down her luggage. She put a dollar in my hand. At first I thought that she gave me the money for the Rainbow Coalition. But then I realized that she gave me the money for bringing down her bag. She thought I was the bellboy."

"Are you serious?" I asked, rather surprised. A bit annoyed, he said, "Yes, of course I'm serious."

His story just reconfirmed what he had been trying to say in so many different ways. Here was a man, virtually a hero on the African continent, who had traveled everywhere in Africa, who had met the Pope, yet in one of the most elegant hotels in New York someone thought he was a bellboy. I remembered his statement, "I do it because I have to. I have to do it for self-respect."

He has campaigned days and nights for candidates who were all white. He pointed out that none of the people who were riding with us in the bus campaigned for him. So why did he do it? Because he knew it would make a difference to black people if these Democrats got elected. "I am trying to build a rainbow coalition. Maybe the next time, they'll return the favor." In some ways, he has been a very patient man.

The campaign bus was filled with local political candidates and their staff. Someone called for a prayer. Pretending to pray, the Reverend Jackson said, "I wish this bus to leave." This was the beginning of a grueling day—getting on the bus, getting off the bus, traveling from one part of the city to another, getting stuck in traffic jams, on an exceptionally nice day in windy Chicago. The mood on the bus was jovial and everyone joked with "The Rev," as some people called him. He started to talk to one of the candidates, but in a matter of moments, there was a deep silence. He had fallen asleep in the middle of the conversation.

As we approached our next stop, the man beside him shook him gently. He awoke quickly, full of energy and ready to go.

We walked into a church filled with people yelling, "Teach, Jesse, teach. Wake us up." He was educating people to go out and vote.

"Now, if you go to the store and they ain't got chicken, and your wife comes back with nothing, wouldn't you say, so what happened to pork chops, hamburgers, or stew? Well, it's the same thing. There's plenty to vote for. It's not just the governor and lieutenant governor, it's the whole slate." Then he offered an analogy. He told them that the Republican candidate was President Reagan's man. Reagan was opposed to sanctions against South Africa, which in Jackson's eyes, meant he was for apartheid. Therefore, the man running on the Republican ticket was for apartheid. He asked his audience, "Would you vote for a man who votes for apartheid in South Africa? Would you vote for him twice? Well, if you vote for Thompson, that's what you are doing."

The actual voting ballot was very confusing, and there was a serious concern about how to explain finding the "right" candidates. Jackson took a glance at the dummy ballot and in a matter of seconds he found a solution. "You vote for 12-41-36, plus judges." Then he would repeat it faster and faster, "12-41-36, plus judges. Twelve is the dozens, 41 is the year I was born or the year that Pearl Harbor was bombed, 36 is what you ladies would all like to be, and don't forget the judges."

The audience laughed as he made them repeat all this over and over again. "Twelve-41-36, plus judges" became the slogan of the day. That was how they were instructed to vote in this election.

Before we left the church hall, as he passed the kitchen he asked an elderly woman what she was cooking. She gave him a piece of fish. That would have been the extent of a meal for him if his lively teenage daughter Jackie had not been campaigning with us. She remembered to bring nuts to munch on and got her father another piece of fish which he swallowed in two bites. He kissed his daughter, commenting to no one in particular, "She loves her daddy!"

Back on the bus, while his daughter sat in the back with a friend, Jackson educated the local politicians on how to win this election. "You got to think BIG." He explained how the media worked; organized a group to call in during a radio talk program to get the message to the people; worked out the strategy for the night before the election; and, in the midst of all this, he instructed the driver how to get out of the traffic and to the next destination.

The audience at the next stop was mostly white. I wondered if the same magic would work on them. The mayor of Chicago, Harold Washington, had been waiting for our bus to arrive. He introduced Jackson with great respect. Jackson did his "12-41-36, plus judges" routine. By the time we left, even the mayor was chanting along. The television cameras were all focused on Jackson. He appeared, at all times, comfortable and relaxed. He made people laugh. For those who were with him on the bus, he made the day fun, though no one would think that spending this kind of day on a bus without eating would be fun.

When Jackson was not taking a nap, he was master-minding each move and every step of the way, like a military commander. What stood out the most about that day was the realization that this man was aware of so much. He would walk into a room and seem to sense everything, with almost terrifying instincts. Time magazine has said, "He can be fascinating and frightening, inspiring and irritating, charismatic and controversial." One saw all that and a bit more.

As we walked through the neighborhood, little children ran up to him. He responded to them in the same warm way that he responded to elderly ladies who wanted to shake his hand. As we crossed a major intersection and the police stopped traffic for our delegation, an old man in a car yelled, "Hey man, hey Jesse." Jackson stopped to say hello and talked to him in an unhurried way as if the world could wait until he was finished. He did not seem fazed by people yelling at him to get across the intersection. He didn't seem to even hear them. The smile on that man's face told the whole story. Talking to this man was more important to him. Why should he care about causing a traffic jam?

Undoubtedly, the one quality about Jackson that stands out is his ability to deal with a diverse group of people. He is able to relate to everyone, and to give a person his undivided attention even if the next moment he is giving directions to the bus driver or asking someone for his peanuts.

Though appearing affluent, with a flamboyant image, he declares himself a man of simple tastes and ordinary desires. He is not the kind of person you could imagine eating in an expensive restaurant or relaxing on a beach. A reporter recalled that when they went to a fancy French restaurant, well known for its exquisite cuisine, Jackson wanted to know if they had spaghetti and meatballs. He flies first class and rides in elegant limousines with several bodyguards, but luxury itself is not important to him. He is always preoccupied with the next move, thinking about how he can convey his messages and how he can organize people who have been left out.

He repeated his deep-rooted feeling that the odds were against him and that he was always fighting them. "I am always trying to think of new ways to get through," he said, pointing to his temple and staring intently at me. He has permitted hundreds of interviews, perhaps in the hope that what he has said will be understood. He has said that he has been misquoted so often, he wonders if anyone really has heard what he was saying, but that he was not really concerned about that because he believed his actions would be judged by God.

A PUBLIC LIFE

Jackson's life is a public one, and he is often away from his family. He and his wife, Jacqueline, and their five children, Jonathan, Santita, Yusef, young Jacqueline, and Jesse, Jr., live in the South Side of Chicago in a Tudor-style house. Jackie traveled with him extensively during his campaign for president, including his trip to Africa. However, for the most part, she has been the anchor in the family, raising their five children, three sons and two daughters, ranging in age from ten to twenty-three.

Jackson has been on the road all the time, seven days a week. When we campaigned all day with his daughter, one of the bodyguards mentioned that it was one of the few ways that his children could spend time with him—on the road, campaigning for one issue or another.

At day's end, those of us who accompanied him on the campaign trail went home, exhausted and hungry, to eat and relax for the night. It was a Saturday night. He went home to change, because that evening he was going to a fund-raiser in another state.

Jackson has lived his life in the public arena, surrounded by important leaders, famous people, bodyguards, and admirers, but his sympathies have been very much with "those who have been locked out."

Jesse and Jacqueline Jackson on the presidential campaign trail in 1983. This photo, showing a hole in his shoe, is reminiscent of a similar photo of Adlai Stevenson taken when he was running for the presidency in the 1950s.

He has made a point of talking to the women who serve in the kitchen or joking with the man in the broken-down car because he apparently identified deeply with the less fortunate.

On the plane back to New York, at the end of a long, exhausting day with Jackson, I thought of a story that one of his staff members had told me, one that stood out, to her, from dozens of others of his campaign.

A few years earlier, Jackson had traveled South to attend an award ceremony for the Girl Scouts. The organizers decided to put the prettiest little girls, all cute and thin, on the podium to sit with Jackson. One girl, less pretty and much heavier, was supposed to sit with him, but the organizers decided at the last minute that since the television cameras were there, they did not want to include a less attractive child. The little girl was on the verge of tears.

As Jackson sat down on the podium, he seemed to sense that something was wrong, that this child was hurt. He stopped the ceremony and asked that an additional chair be squeezed onto the stage. At first the organizers didn't understand why. Then he pointed to the little girl and asked her to come and sit right next to him. The organizers were dismayed. Why this ugly, fat kid, they seemed to be thinking.

When it was time for photos to be taken, he picked up the child and kissed her, which was the picture that was published in the newspapers. Jackson's staff member heard him whisper, "Don't let them ever break your spirit. Don't let them get you down." The photograph of the child in Jackson's arms was hung on the wall of her home.

"Jackson probably doesn't even remember this story. He does this kind of thing all the time. But that child will remember. She'll never forget the impact he had on her life. I bet you she probably even lost weight after that. He's always for the underdog," said the staff member.

8

Jackson's Impact on American Life

To sum up Jackson's impact on American life is a difficult task. First and foremost, he has been an educator—an advocate for justice and a consistent fighter for equality, dignity, and peace.

As one of his long-time staff members observed, "You cannot think of the last twenty years without considering the 'Jesse factor.' He has been involved with every major political and social issue. That's why, when he ran for president, we had such high name recognition. America has been looking at him on television for twenty years."

Undoubtedly, he has been in the forefront of the civil rights movement, articulating the needs and conditions of disadvantaged blacks. Whether he is talking about educating people to vote, or organizing economic boycotts, or explaining the issue of apartheid, above all, through the years, he has projected the aspirations of black Americans to the world. He has been their most significant advocate for self-respect, pride, and excellence. He offered a psychological replenishment for people whose spirit had been broken.

We have read on the front page of the *New York Times* that because of his leadership, black voters have made an impact in the South. They will be the deciding factor in the outcome of numerous elections. The *New York Times* reported, "Thirty years ago, in the bayous of Louisiana and the cotton fields of Mississippi and other Southern states, it was unthinkable that a black would run for a seat in Congress, never mind stand a chance of winning." And few would have believed that the day would come when blacks, who were by and large barred from voting by well-enforced Jim Crow laws, would be in a position to help determine who won or lost an election.

This could be called the "Jesse factor." He has changed the shape of the political composition of America. The black vote counts, and the candidates understand their impact. No one suggests that Jackson did it alone. However, he played a major role in advocating that a black vote was something that all candidates must concern themselves with in a serious way if they wanted to win.

Jackson also demonstrated that the campaign against drugs must consider the user as well as the pusher. He has expressed the view that hopelessness and despair lead to drug use. If people have the need to use drugs, they will find the supplier. He has turned attention to the youth, spreading the message that they must take responsibility for their own actions. Much of the national anticrack campaign took its model from his emphasis on the individual—"Just say no."

He has played no small part in educating the American public about apartheid as it has been influenced by American business involvement in South Africa. On September 29, 1986, the United States Congress passed a resolution imposing sanctions against South Africa, and in response, conglomerates like IBM and General Motors, along with numerous other companies, ceased to do business there. Also, several states have been withdrawing their interest in that country, a move which Jackson has been advocating for years.

Jackson, of course, has not been alone in protesting the policies of the South African government. Several organizations, including Transafrica, in Washington, D.C., have been working on exposing the suffering in South Africa caused by its system of racial separation. However, Jackson, during his presidential campaign, raised this issue whenever he had the opportunity. He became a champion of that cause.

As one journalist put it, "He is no longer a black leader, but rather he is an all-purpose leader." While it is true that in the sixties he served as a champion and a major spokesman for the black cause, today his words represent a broader constituency. He has talked about the Rainbow Coalition as a major commitment in his life. And in the spirit of that concept, he has campaigned for both black and white candidates. In the reception area of the National Rainbow Coalition's headquarters in Washington, D.C., there is a painting consisting of all the colors of the rainbow—a symbol of his vision. The staff, many of whom have worked with him for fifteen to twenty years, have been white and black. The only picture of him on the wall is one with a Syrian child, again reflecting his international concerns.

"You know, having Jesse around is like driving on a highway late at night. There is a natural tendency to speed. But you don't really dare, because you know that the police will get you. Jesse is like the watchdog that's always there. He's on top of everything. He'll remind you if the country has done something wrong," recalled a staff member.

It is important to remember that many people who were in the civil rights movement in the 1960s have died or gave up the struggle a long time ago, a number entering the mainstream of America, no longer dedicating their lives to issues of justice or equality.

But twenty years later, Jackson is still hammering away at the core of the problem—the violation of human rights. He has said he still believes that the American system is worth improving, and that he believes in democracy and the power of the vote. He still works hard, speaking out on matters of public concern, marching for peace, campaigning for other candidates, or talking to the young people about issues that affect them.

Many adversaries regard him as a media "junkie" who likes to be in the public eye. One of his staff members has said, however, "It may be true that he likes to be on the tube, but that does not take away from the fact that it's still work. He is working when he talks to the press. He is still talking about issues."

On March 19, 1987, Jackson opened a campaign office in Iowa, beginning his effort to explore a possible second race for the presidency. According to the New York Times, Jackson is expected to make a major effort in Iowa, where hard-pressed farmers appear to be a receptive audience for his attacks on "economic royalism."

If Jackson does run for the presidency, his campaign would remind America that a black man was challenging America's readiness to accept all people and embrace all colors and ethnic groups equally. No one can predict what might happen. Even if he didn't win the election, he would again inspire other black Americans to run for political office. Someday, a black person might be elected president. If that should happen, Jesse Jackson's name will not be forgotten.

Africans regard Jackson as a hero. They hope he will help solve some of the problems confronting that continent. No one, with the exception of former U.N. Ambassador Andrew Young, has reached that status or recognition. He is an outsider, yet the people of Africa consider him their son. He is Africa's unofficial

Jesse Jackson, at a march in Stanford,
California, in honor of Martin Luther King, Jr.'s
birthday on January 15, 1987, shows off
an antiapartheid shirt to a group of children.

ambassador to America, helping to educate the American public about Africa.

Jackson has never compromised his principles or let anyone break his spirit. If he never did another thing, he still will have accomplished more than most people do in their entire lifetime. Yet he is still a young man; he has many more years to pursue his dream of a Rainbow Coalition.

Though he is disliked by some, few would claim that they don't respect the endless struggle that he has waged to educate, to teach the young, to preach and talk about self-respect and dignity for all Americans. He has said, "I was made aware of the odds of survival as a child. I'm still fighting those odds and denying those odds."

Sources

In writing this book, I drew upon interviews I had with the Reverend Jesse Jackson; former and current members of his staff, particularly his long-time associate Jack O'Dell; journalists; political adversaries; and colleagues. Much of my knowledge of the civil rights movement of the 1960s was acquired first-hand as producer of *Night Call*, a nationwide radio program, during which I interviewed most of those in the forefront of that movement.

I am indebted to Roger Wilkins for his objective critique of this manuscript and for his helpful suggestions.

In addition I relied on the following books and articles:

BOOKS

Reed, Adolph L., Jr. *The Jesse Jackson Phenomenon.* New Haven, Connecticut: Yale University Press, 1986.

Reynolds, Barbara A. *Jesse Jackson: America's David.* (Published in 1975 as *Jesse Jackson: The Man, The Movement, The Myth.*) Washington, D.C.: JFJ Associates, 1985.

Stone, Eddie. *Jesse Jackson.* Los Angeles: Holloway House, 1979.

ARTICLES

"America's 15 Greatest Black Preachers." *Ebony,* September 1984, 27.

Anderson, Kurt. "Jackson Plays by the Rules: A Good Soldier—but Drafting His Own Battle Plan." *Time,* November 5, 1984, 29.

Ball, Joanne. "Fighting for Economic Parity." *Black Enterprise,* November 1983, 50.

"Black Democrats Assail Plan." *New York Times,* March 6, 1986, 13.

Cassese, Sid. "Jesse Jackson: the Leader of PUSH urges Boycotts for Dollars Power." *Essence,* June 1983, 14.

Church, George J. "What Does Jesse Really Want?" *Time,* April 16, 1984, 15.

Coverson, Laura. "A PUSH for Heublein." *Black Enterprise,* June 1982, 50.

Delaney, Paul. "Voting: the New Black Power." *New York Times Magazine,* November 27, 1983, 34.

Drew, Elizabeth. "A Political Journal." *New Yorker,* May 28, 1984, 104.

Edwards, Audrey. "Winning with Jesse." *Essence,* July 1984, 72.

Fineman, Howard. "Promises, Promises." *Newsweek,* January 9, 1984, 32.

Green, Philip. "The Reality Beneath the Rainbow: Why I'm for Jackson." *Nation,* March 17, 1984, 305.

"Jackson and the Jews." Editorial. *New Republic,* March 19, 1984, 9.

"The Jackson Factor." *Economist,* July 21, 1984, 23.

"The Jackson Factor." Editorial. *Nation,* April 14, 1984, 433.

"Jackson in Cuba." *Black Enterprise,* September 1984, 18.

"Jesse and George." *National Review,* June 29, 1984, 13.

"Jesse Jackson: Black Charisma on the Campaign Trail." *Ebony,* August 1984, 92.

"Jesse Jackson, Diplomat." *National Review,* June 14, 1985, 15.

Kirshenbaum, Jerry. "Semirhymed Parallelisms." *Sports Illustrated,* June 6, 1983, 28.

Kopkind, Andrew. "Black Power in the Age of Jackson." *Nation,* November 26, 1983, 521.

Leerhsen, Charles. "Special Coverage for Jesse?" *Newsweek,* April 9, 1984, 72.

Meyers, John A. "Interviewing Jesse Jackson." *Time,* August 22, 1983, 1.

"The New Gospel According to PUSH." *Newsweek,* August 16, 1982, 52.

Pierce, Kenneth M. "A Mixed Bag from Fidel's Jails: Dope Dealers and Dissidents Are Among Jesse's 48 Freed Men." *Time,* July 9, 1984, 11.

"The Rainbow Continues to Grow—It Takes Time." *US News and World Report*, April 23, 1984, 34.

"Rainbow's End." Editorial. *New Republic*, April 30, 1984, 7.

"Rainbow Without End." *Economist*, June 9, 1984, 23.

Reeves, Richard. "New Ideas Shape Presidential Politics." *New York Times Magazine*, July 15, 1984, 26.

Ruffin, David C. "New-style Politics: from Grass Roots to Mainstream." *Black Enterprise*, August 1985, 114.

Ruffin, David C., and Derek T. Dingle. "Forging Coalitions." *Black Enterprise*, October 1984, 23.

Shapiro, Walter, and Howard Fineman. "The Democrats' End Game; Hart Remains the Odd Man Out as Mondale and Jackson Begin to Make Peace." *Newsweek*, May 14, 1984, 20.

Strasser, Steven. "Jesse Jackson and the Jews." *Newsweek*, March 5, 1984, 26.

"A Talk with Jesse Jackson." *Newsweek*, April 9, 1984, 35.

"Taking Jackson Seriously." *New York Times Magazine*, May 14, 1984, 24.

Toner, Robin. "For Jesse Jackson, a Campaign to Stay Visible." *New York Times*, December 9, 1985, 12.

"Where Democratic Candidates Stand." *US News and World Report*, May 28, 1984, 55.

White, Theodore H. "The Shaping of the Presidency 1984." *Time*, November 19, 1984, 70.

Wiley, Jean. "Beyond '84: Keep Moving! Jackson's Rainbow: Here to Stay!" *Essence*, November 1984, 16.

Wilkins, Roger. "The Natural." *Mother Jones*, August-September 1984, 40.

Williams, Jean. "PUSH Backing Promoters: Jackson Moves to End White Monopoly." *Billboard*, January 30, 1982, 1.

Woodward, Kenneth L. "Tough Rules of Brotherhood." *Newsweek*, July 16, 1984, 80.

Index

A & P supermarkets, boycott of, 35–36
Abernathy, Dr. Ralph, 12, 26, 32, 42
Affirmative action, 70
Africa, 80–83, 100
Agriculture and Technical College of North Carolina at Greensboro, 24
American life, impact on, 97–102
American social system, youth and, 49
American society, moral decay of, 52
American youth, as a priority, 52
Apartheid, 80, 88
Attitude, importance of, 52

Baseball, major league offers to play, 24
Black Americans, impact on aspirations of, 97
Black banks, investment in, 35

Black business, development of, 35
Black capitalism, 33
Black Christmas, 54–56
Black community, 35–36
Black consumers, 33
Black Enterprise, 55
Black Expo, 41–44
Black mayors, emergence of, 59–61
Black ministers, 29
Black Muslims, 68
Black Panthers, 14
Black power, use of money as, 54
Black Pride, 54
Black Soul Saint, 55
Boycotts, 24–26, 34–36, 97
Burns, Helen, 17

Campaigns, 89–94
Candidacy for president, 1984, 63–73
    black leaders opposition to, 66–69

Central America, 83–84
Chicago
 desegration, 29–31
 ghettos, 53–61
 King, Dr. Martin Luther,
  Jr., 27–31
 political scene, 58–61
 riots, 1963, 13
 segregation, 28–31
 student days, 27
Chicago Theological Seminary,
 25
Chicago White Sox, 24
Childhood, 19–22
Chisholm, Shirley, 57
Citizen groups, role in deseg-
 regation, 30
Civil economics movement,
 46
Civil rights movement, 11–17,
 27, 97
College years, 24–26
Congress of Racial Equality
 (CORE), 24
Christmas boycott, 54
Convention delegates, increase
 in black members as, 71
Country Delight, boycott of, 34
Cuba, 78–80

Daley, Richard, 28–31
Democratic Convention, 1972,
 56–78
 Jackson's address to, 73
Democratic National Conven-
 tion Credentials Commis-
 sion, 1972, 57
Democratic party, conflict of
 Jackson's candidacy and,
 66–69
Desegration, Jackson's role in,
 11–17, 27, 29–31. See also
 Civil rights
Drugs, campaign against, 98

Economic boycotts, 97. See
 also Boycotts
Economic gains, blacks and,
 33
Economic structure, black integration into, 33
Education
 black consumers and, 33
 importance of, 49
 of local politicians, 92
 parental involvement in,
  47
Equal Opportunity, support of,
 70
Equal Rights Amendment
 (ERA), 70

Family and home life, 17–22,
 94–97
Farrakhan, Louis, 68
Foreign affairs
 policies since 1984, 75–85
 position in 1984 campaign,
  70
Front Line states, pilgrimage
 to, 83
"Fruits of Islam" bodyguards,
 68

"Gay rights," 70
Global issues, 84–85
Goodman, Lt. R.O., Jr., 75–78
Grandparents, 17
Greenville, S.C., family home,
 17

Health problems, 87
High school years, 22–24
Honduras, 83–84
Human rights, 64, 100
Hunger, position on, 84

"I am somebody," 38, 52